FACILITATIVE LEADERSHIP

*Managing Performance
without Controlling People*

STEVE REILLY

Seattle, Washington
Portland, Oregon
Denver, Colorado
Vancouver, B.C.

Library of Congress No. 96-069001
Steve Reilly

IBSN 0-89716-620-5

Cover design: David Marty
Production: Malia A. Johnson

Second Printing June 2001

PEANUT BUTTER PUBLISHING

PEANUT BUTTER PUBLISHING
2207 FAIRVIEW AVENUE EAST
HOUSEBOAT NUMBER FOUR
SEATTLE WASHINGTON 98102
206-860-4900

e mail: pnutpub@aol.com

Printed in Canada

ing to them. In both situations, the manager, not the employee, is responsible for ensuring performance.

The autocratic behaviorist model for managing people works well in a hierarchical, structured environment in which roles and responsibilities are static and clearly defined, such as the military. This model works well in the military because decision making is top-down and highly structured. Up until recently, the military and corporate organizational structures mirrored each other. Because the environments were similar, autocratic behaviorism worked well as a management philosophy in both.

Today however, the role of the corporate manager is rapidly becoming blurred and more difficult to define, much like the structures of today's corporations. The environment and underlying assumptions that once supported the autocratic behaviorist model have changed.

In the past, management was primarily responsible for making decisions. In today's corporations, non-managers are expected to make decisions that were traditionally made by managers. The common management belief in our modern business environment is that decisions are best made by the people closest to the customer. This belief has impacted management's role.

Additionally, managers are responsible for more people today than in the past. Managers used to be able to count the number of people they were responsible for on one hand. The flatter, leaner corporate model means more non-managers reporting to less managers. This has complicated managers' jobs and put increased pressure on their time.

The changing organizational structure has also impacted a manager's role. Corporate structures are making the transition from stable and predictable to flexible and adaptive. With this change, managers are expected to be more flexible as well.

If managers are going to be successful in this new, complex environment it will not be by trying to gain more control over people. It will be by learning to manage without control.

Acknowledgements

This book is for anyone who has worked for an unfair boss. It is also for anyone who has been an unfair boss.

The concepts taught in this book are the result of many mistakes. Some mistakes made by me, some made by people who managed me. Unfortunately, for some of the people I managed, these concepts and skills were learned by trial and error.

In this book, I have tried to provide a framework which clearly defines a manager's responsibilities to the people he or she manages. This framework is a structure for managers to organize their thinking so they can fulfill those responsibilities. My hope is by reading this book, applying the concepts and practicing the skills, managers will take on a leadership role by building a foundation which encourages self-management.

I owe this book to every manager who fired me and every person I fired. I owe it also to the parents who raised me and the daughter I am raising.

But most of all I am indebted to my wife, Astrid. She taught me the most important lesson without which this book would not be possible. I learned from her that the more you try to control another person, the less he or she will be committed to you. That is a lesson I can apply to managing people, raising a child or loving a wife.

It is also the key lesson in this book.

Contents

Chapter 3

Chapter 4
Accountability

Chapter 5
Can Facilitative Leadership Work in the American Business Culture?

Introduction

In the American business culture, the most prevalent approach to managing people is "autocratic behaviorism." Autocratic behaviorism is defined as using positional authority to control people's actions. The hallmark of an autocratic behaviorist management culture is a focus on controlling behavior through systems of rewards and punishments. Employees are rewarded for good behavior and punished for poor behavior. This management approach is in response to and reinforced by our short-term, bottom line business environment.

Autocratic behaviorism is typically applied by managers with one of two different management styles. These styles are referred to as either "hands off" or "hands on" management.

"Hands off" refers to managers who avoid controlling until they have to. The term "hands on" applies to those managers who actively try to control people's behavior.

Most "hands off" managers abdicate their people-management responsibilities until negative performance issues arise. When forced to deal with an employee's negative behavior, a "hands off" manager uses rewards or punishments as tools to control or correct. These rewards or punishments consist of inducements for positive results and "accountability" for negative results.

The "hands on" manager takes a different approach to control behavior. "Hands on" managers often try to exert control in areas over which they have little or no control. These managers actively use rewards and punishments to get people to behave in a certain way.

Both "hands off" and "hands on" managers use different styles in applying the same autocratic behaviorist approach. "If you do this, you get that. If you don't do this, this will happen to you." When employees perform well, management makes sure they get what is coming to them and when employees perform poorly, management makes sure they get what is com-

Management's New Role

Autocratic behaviorism worked well in an environment in which managers had the time and authority to make decisions for their people. In the current business environment this approach interferes with success. Managers no longer have the time or power to control employee behavior. Nor do they want to. This new environment demands that employees learn to "self-manage."

Management's role has shifted from ensuring that people fulfill their duties and meet objectives to helping people take responsibility and make smart decisions. This shifts a manager's role from controlling behavior to helping people become better decision makers. This shift is from autocratic behaviorism to facilitative leadership. To be successful, managers need to facilitate the process of building confidence in their people's decision making abilities.

In the autocratic behaviorist model, a manager would measure success by how much confidence employees had in his or her abilities. A facilitative leader measures success by the amount of confidence his or her employees have in their own abilities. In this new environment, a manager's primary responsibility is to help people build their confidence.

When people have confidence in their ability to make smart decisions, they will self-manage. In order for people to become confident in their decision making, they must be allowed to make decisions. Management's duty is to help people learn to make smart decisions by creating a safe environment in which people have opportunities to make decisions. This is not about control. It is about learning. Management's new role is to facilitate the learning process.

This new role requires both management and leadership skills. A facilitative leader creates and manages the opportunities for employees to learn to become responsible decision makers. The task of building this environment requires a shift in how managers view their job.

From Profits to Process

The business value most reinforced in American corporate culture is results. Management gets rewarded for achieving results and making profits. The over-emphasis on results has a strong influence on how managers view their job. The dominance of our short-term, results-driven value system manifests itself in the American "just do it" management culture. In this culture, managers see that their primary responsibility is to achieve results. This is reflected in management practices. Management doesn't reward people for incremental improvements. Management rewards people for meeting objectives and achieving goals.

From this "just do it" culture arises the primary misconception impacting the American management approach: the belief that results can be managed. That setting goals and holding people accountable is managing. This is not managing. It is an attempt to manage results.

Results cannot be managed. People and companies either achieve or fall short of results. Set-

ting goals or objectives and using accountability to motivate lets management off the hook
from actually having to manage. No one can
manage results. A person can only manage
process.

Managing people's progress has not traditionally been very high on the list of American
business values. The over-emphasis on
achievement allows managers to use results as
the measure of how well they are at managing.
This results-focused mentality interferes with a
manager's ability to focus on the process of
managing.

Another complication of the "just do it" management culture is how managers view performance problems. Managers who define an
employee's success by achievement of results
will define an employee's failure as falling
short of results. Employee performance is rated
in terms of achievement, not improvement.
Performance is rated relative to the end-result,
so a manager naturally sees the employee as the
source of the performance problem. The employee is perceived as failing, not the management process. The employee, not the manager,
has fallen short of the goal.

When the employee is perceived as the source of the problem, managers will try to "fix" the employee. They default to an autocratic behaviorist approach. Managers who see employees as the problem have no other recourse than to use a control-based approach to try and correct the problem. In the end, employees end up feeling controlled because they are being controlled.

There is an alternative to the autocratic behaviorist approach: the facilitative approach. In order to better understand how these approaches differ and to further comprehend the underlying assumptions of each, we will analyze how managers using each approach would attempt to solve a people problem, a problem of non-performance.

A
Performance
Problem

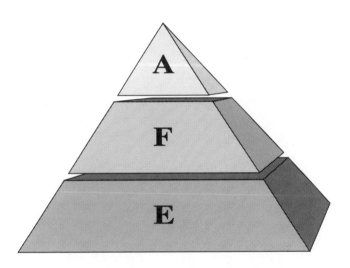

Chapter 1:

A Performance Problem

Imagine you are a manager who inherits an employee from another department in your company. His name is Bob. Bob is one of the poorest performers, and it is your job to turn him around. This is Bob's last chance. If you succeed in correcting his problems, you will receive a substantial bonus and Bob keeps his job. If you fail to improve his performance, you lose the bonus and Bob loses his job.

This afternoon you have an appointment with Bob. This will be the first opportunity to start the process of turning Bob around; the first chance to help salvage his career. In preparation for the meeting you sit down and try to determine where to start.

Looking into Bob's personnel file, you dis-
cover a litany of problems recorded by his
previous manager. They include:

- He is consistently late for work about 2
  days per month.

- Bob failed to accomplish his objectives
  in the previous fiscal year.

- He doesn't return voice mail messages
  for days.

- He constantly bothers other employees
  when they are busy.

- He shows up late for meetings, even the
  meetings he calls.

- He invades other people's offices to chat,
  even when his projects are overdue.

- He refuses to deal with certain employees.

- He has alienated many employees to the
  point where they no longer deal with
  him.

Where do you start? You ask yourself some
questions: Is Bob the right person for the job?
Is he motivated to do the job? Why does he

seem to create his own problems? Does he have an attitude problem? Is his personal life interfering with his performance?

When faced with this problem, managers try to figure out whether or not Bob wants to do the job, and whether he is or isn't motivated to change his behaviors. If Bob isn't motivated they will then try to "fix" Bob by motivating him. Most managers feel that if a person isn't motivated, there is little that can be done to turn around poor performance. Following this route, managers who fail to motivate Bob will most likely attempt to replace him with someone who is motivated.

This strategy of trying to motivate employees, and if unsuccessful hiring someone else, is another attempt to manage results, not process. All managers want employees who are right for the job and motivated. Managers believe they have most control over these two factors: selection and motivation. They attempt to manage performance problems by trying to motivate employees, and failing that, look for someone who can and will do the job. Managers think they can avoid the responsibility of managing if they hire qualified, motivated people.

Unfortunately, motivation and selection are the two factors over which managers have the least control. Using these factors to try and solve a performance problem is a simplistic approach to a more complex problem.

In order to determine what strategy a facilitative leader might take, we must understand the factors that influence the ability of a person to perform a task.

Human Performance Factors

The ability of a person to perform a task is influenced by six factors. Managers have more control over some of these factors than others.

The six factors that influence performance are listed below in descending order of the amount of control a manager has over them.

1. Expectations:

Has the employee been told explicitly what is expected by his or her manager and company?

2. Feedback:

Does the employee know whether he or she is or is not meeting the defined expectations?

3. Accountability:

Has the employee experienced both positive and negative consequences of his behavior?

4. Resources:

Does the employee have everything he or she needs to meet expectations?

5. Selection:

Is the employee the right person for the job?

6. Motivation:

Does the employee want to do the job?

At this point the reader might be hesitant to accept the order of these factors. That is natural. This resistance comes from the tendency in this country to focus on outcome and not process; our "just do it" culture. The outcome Bob's manager wants from this management challenge is an employee who is right for the job and motivated. How a manager gets Bob there is process.

Because of the focus on outcomes rather than process, managers address problems after they have occurred, not before. This focus influences how managers see and deal with performance problems. They most often see the employee and not themselves as the problem. Upon seeing the employee as the problem, managers try to correct it by attempting to motivate.

Managers who try to motivate or terminate employees without doing the groundwork are trying to manage results. They believe they have more control over employee hiring and motivation than they actually do.

The groundwork for facilitating learning is established by addressing the performance factors which are most important and over which managers have the most control.

The Three Most Critical Performance Factors

1. Expectations:

Most managers in this country do a poor job of communicating and reaching agreement on clear expectations. When expectations are unclear it is unfair to try and hold people accountable. Holding people accountable to unclear expectations is like asking a person to play a game without knowing the rules and enforcing all penalties. Managers who assume employees know what is expected and then attempt to hold them accountable are not managing. They are using accountability as a means to control behavior.

The first step in turning around Bob's performance is to ensure that he understands what is expected of him. Bob deserves clear expectations. You cannot expect an employee to take responsibility for his or her actions unless he or she knows what is expected.

Managers who do set expectations often do it in an autocratic way. Expectations can be set as hard and fast rules or as boundaries within which people can make their own decisions. Expectations can be set in a way that facilitates the learning process. The way expectations are set can be the starting point for helping people become better decision makers.

2. Feedback:

Most managers in this country resist giving employees prompt, frequent feedback. They use the yearly performance appraisal process as a way to avoid interaction on a regular basis.

Managers owe employees feedback. Without feedback, employees are operating in the dark and will often create their own. A manager's role is to provide information that allows employees to know how they are doing and whether or not they are improving.

Bob needs to know where he stands in relation to management's expectations. Without feedback how can Bob be expected to improve his performance?

Most managers who provide feedback do so in an attempt to control behavior; positive feedback for good behavior and negative feedback for poor behavior. There is an alternative. Feedback can be used as a tool for facilitating a person's learning process instead of as a means to control.

3. Accountability:

Managers owe employees accountability. This may sound strange, but managers who continually let people off the hook or interfere with the direct consequences of people's actions prevent them from learning. Some managers have a tendency to over-use accountability as a stick to get people to fall in line. Others avoid it at all costs. Both approaches to holding people accountable fall into the autocratic behaviorist model.

If Bob's manager has provided him with a solid basis of clear expectations and frequent feedback, then Bob has chosen to live with the consequences of his actions. Unfortunately, managers who do a poor job of providing clear expectations and feedback often use accountability as a method to control behavior. They substitute accountability for managing.

Accountability can be another tool for people

to become better decision makers. It depends on how it is used. In order for people to become better decision makers they must have the opportunity to make decisions and experience the direct consequences of those decisions. Facilitating the learning process means providing a safe environment for people to make decisions and experience consequences. It means helping people to hold themselves accountable.

Managers owe their employees clear expectations, frequent feedback and accountability. How a manager provides these three is the difference between autocratic behaviorism and facilitative leadership.

A Manager's Span of Control

A famous conductor once said, "When I have a problem with the orchestra, I come down off my podium, walk into my dressing room and look in the mirror. I usually find the source of the problem staring back at me." This statement embodies the difference between facilitation and control.

Managers who attempt to control behavior will place their emphasis on accountability to get people to do what they want. These managers see their role in providing clear expectations and frequent feedback as less important than accountability.

The facilitative leader sees that his or her primary responsibility is to provide expectations and feedback. Doing a good job of clarifying expectations and giving feedback reduces the need to hold people accountable.

In general, managers in this country emphasize accountability over expectations and feedback. Recently a trend has developed for managers to engineer more accountability into the workplace. There are three reasons for this increasing emphasis on accountability.

The primary reason is the "just do it" management approach. This puts primary emphasis on results, not process. Managers are good at identifying goals and objectives but not very good at clarifying expectations and providing feedback. Unfortunately, this ability interferes with managing the progress towards achieving those goals. Management-by-Objectives is not managing; it is goal setting. It is another attempt to manage results.

Second, most managers are unclear on their roles and responsibilities. Corporations send their managers to leadership seminars before they have the skills to do an effective job of managing. It is very difficult to become a good leader without management skills. With the increase in authority that people get when promoted into management goes an increase in responsibility to the people they manage. When managers only see the increase in authority without feeling the increased responsibility, they will use accountability to exercise that authority.

The third reason managers focus on accountability to manage is the fast paced, results-focused environment they work in. This environment encourages management by exception. The squeaky wheel gets the oil. Managing by exception focuses on solving problems after they have occurred. Managers naturally see the employee as the cause of the problem.

A person who is interested in facilitating the learning process builds the groundwork for people to make decisions. He or she first realizes the increased responsibility, then the increased authority.

The first and most important step for facilitating the learning process is to provide clear expectations. Expectations create the base camp from which people can push themselves to greater heights. Expectations provide the net which makes it safe to take risks. Facilitative leaders accept the responsibility of ensuring that people have a good foundation for achievement.

The second most important step of facilitating the learning process is to frequently provide feedback. Feedback helps people manage their own progress. Facilitative leaders spend time giving feedback about how a person is improving or slipping in their progress. This feedback is process-based more than results-based. Results-based feedback identifies whether an employee has or hasn't achieved an objective. Process-based feedback reinforces specific behaviors that are or are not working. Using the base camp analogy, reaching the summit is a good goal, but most people appreciate help determining the best equipment and route to get to the top.

When a solid base of expectations exists and people know how they are doing in relation to those expectations, then accountability becomes a natural part of the process. As people become more confident in their decision making abilities they are more likely to hold themselves accountable. Facilitative leadership doesn't mean holding people accountable. It means helping people hold themselves accountable. A leader doesn't try to make people responsible; he or she helps people take responsibility.

Shifting away from an autocratic behaviorist approach is not accomplished by doing different things. It is achieved by shifting the primary emphasis away from the employee's actions to the manager's responsibilities in helping or hindering a person's success. Facilitating learning means focusing on the parts of the process which managers have control over and are responsible for providing to their employees. The manager looks first in the mirror for the source of the problem.

The difference between an autocratic behaviorist approach and that of the facilitative leader can be illustrated in the models below. A manager who attempts to control behavior uses accountability as his or her primary tool. Feedback is usually in the form of a performance appraisal or infrequent "constructive" criticism. Expectations are assumed.

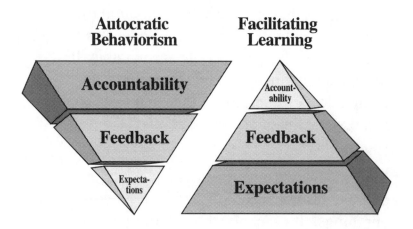

Facilitating learning requires a different emphasis than a control-based approach. The facilitative leader sees his or her primary role as communicating, clarifying and coming to agreement on the boundaries within which all employees are expected to work. Feedback is process- and results-based. When clear, agreed upon expectations exist and prompt, frequent feedback has been given, employees hold themselves accountable. Facilitative leaders get themselves out of the way.

This shift in emphasis also requires a different way of providing expectations, feedback and accountability. Managers can provide these three factors to their people in a way that doesn't attempt to control them. Before we move onto this topic, it is important to clarify how much control managers have over the three remaining performance factors: resources, selection and motivation.

Resources, Selection and Motivation

Most managers do not have direct control over resources. Very often resources like supplies and equipment must be requisitioned from other parts of the organization. This requires other decision makers over whom managers have less control. One resource a manager does have more control over is his or her time. Accessibility to his or her manager is a very important factor in a person's development.

Many managers believe they have control over selection through the hiring and firing process. The thought process behind this belief is flawed. Any manager who has out-placed an employee for a performance problem has experienced the process of putting that employee on a performance plan.

The performance plan helps protect a company from the legal liability of firing an employee without justification. In order to protect a company all performance plans incorporate the same process: to formalize and document that the employee was provided with clear expectations, prompt feedback and equitable accountability. It is unfortunate for employees that these three critical factors are used as a way to terminate rather than a way to help at the beginning of the process.

Finally, managers think they can motivate people. While there are managers whom employees consider motivational, if people don't want to be motivated there is little a manager can do. Managers who are seen as motivational by their people usually have a good record of providing clear expectations, offering frequent feedback and being fair and equitable. When people have this firm foundation they are more likely to motivate themselves.

Traditionally, motivation has been a primary focus of management training in this country. Management believes that motivation is the answer to many performance problems. To understand why, we need to take a look at the two types of motivation and their effects.

Extrinsic Vs. Intrinsic Motivations

There are two different types of motivations that influence behavior: intrinsic and extrinsic. Factors which extrinsically motivate come from outside the person. Intrinsic motivation comes from within the person.

The main extrinsic motivators used in the American business culture are rewards and punishments. Extrinsic rewards can take many forms, such as money, recognition and praise. Examples of punishments are criticism, withholding rewards and reprimand.

Extrinsic motivators come from someone or some organization extrinsic to or outside of the person. Because they are things "done to" the person, extrinsic motivators are used to control people's behavior. The underlying premise is that if you do what the manager or company wants then you get rewarded; if you don't, you don't.

Extrinsic motivators do motivate. They motivate people to do what others want them to do.

They build dependent behavior because the person being "motivated" depends on the person delivering the extrinsic motivator to determine whether he or she has behaved in the desired way. Managers who use extrinsic motivators build management-dependent behavior.

Intrinsic motivators are internally defined by a person. They self-motivate. Intrinsic motivators are things a person finds interesting and likes to do. They are done for their own sake, not for someone else's. They can be an individual's sense of achievement and improvement or the desire to learn or be part of a group.

Intrinsic motivators are not controlled by outside forces; people motivate themselves. Intrinsic motivators become stronger in environments in which people have more control over their choices. They weaken when people feel controlled. Extrinsic motivators become stronger the more they are used because people come to expect them.

The over-reliance on extrinsic motivators is a symptom of an autocratic behaviorist management approach. Managers who rely on extrinsic motivators to control behavior usually end up

with people who rely on managers to provide
extrinsic motivators. By focusing on the end
result, managers create an environment in
which their people focus on the end result: the
reward. Thus managers create management-
dependent behavior.

In the remaining chapters we will use Bob to
contrast a management approach that empha-
sizes control to one that facilitates learning.
Chapter Two will examine expectations and
how managers can either create an environment
in which people self-manage or one which
reinforces management-dependent behavior.
Chapter Three identifies the different effects of
results-based and process-based feedback. In
the fourth chapter two different methods for
helping people hold themselves accountable
are presented.

The final chapter deals with the problem of
empowerment. It illustrates how today's corporate environment works against empowerment
and a game plan for moving to an empowered
workplace is offered. The objective of the rest
of this book is to help managers shift from
trying to control behavior to helping people
improve their decision making skills.

To make this shift managers will need to focus on the three critical performance factors: expectations, feedback and accountability.

Expectations

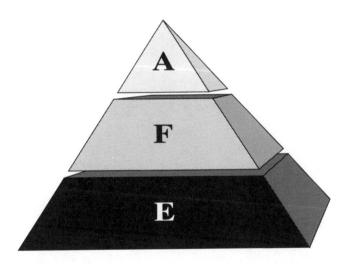

Chapter 2:

Expectations

Does Bob know explicitly what is expected of him by his manager and company?

S o there you are, one hour before your meeting with Bob to try and turn around his performance. There are a number of documented complaints about Bob's performance left in a file by his previous manager. You want to make sure to address those that will impact Bob and his contribution to the department the most. In his file you identify three complaints on which to focus.

First, Bob is consistently late for work an average of two days out of each month. Co-workers complain that this behavior interferes with their ability to hold early meetings. Also, those who depend on Bob's work are upset that they can't reach him at critical times.

Second, Bob doesn't return voice mail messages for days. When he does finally answer them he often leaves incomplete or abrupt answers.

Third, Bob only partially met his objective last year of introducing two new products to the market. He did introduce one new product, but it didn't meet customer requirements. He never got around to introducing the second product.

Bob's previous manager left some notes in Bob's file concerning his responses to these problems. Regarding his chronic lateness, Bob is a single parent and has a problem with his daycare. The daycare sometimes falls through and he has to make last-minute arrangements.

About the voice mail issue, Bob feels overworked. When his manager tried to hold him accountable Bob pointed out that it sometimes took his manager a long time to answer voice mail messages. Bob also indicated that he likes to wait until he has all the information necessary before returning a message.

When asked why he only introduced one product to the market during the previous year, Bob said that the marketing department didn't get the research data to him in time to introduce more than one product. Additionally, he stated that the product which was introduced met all the internal specifications before release. He felt that it wasn't his fault if the market research was wrong.

As Bob's manager, where do you start? How do you define and clarify expectations for Bob without controlling him? How do you use expectations to facilitate the learning process while meeting your objectives?

To answer these questions we have to look at the underlying assumptions managers have about expectations.

Understanding Expectations

Most managers do a poor job of communicating expectations. They often assume that people should know the proper rules of conduct. Many think everyone has or should have the same value system as they or their company. Another contributing factor may be that managers find it easier to manage by exception to avoid potential conflicts which might arise from defining expectations. The last reason managers do a poor job of setting expectations is that they often don't know what they need to communicate.

In addressing the first reason, it is important to realize that assumptions are dangerous. As anyone who has had to defend the firing of an employee knows, the first and most important question asked by legal counsel is "Did you explicitly tell your employee that this was part of his or her job?" The manager will have to answer that question with a simple "yes" or "no." Assumptions won't work.

Managers who avoid setting expectations because of potential conflict may do so because of their underlying belief system about expectations. If managers perceive expectations as rules and regulations established by management and imposed upon employees, then it is understandable that they avoid them. If, however, managers perceive and set expectations as boundaries jointly agreed upon and implemented to facilitate efficient work processes, then there is less of a reason to fear conflict. Rules and regulations are meant to control; boundaries provide guidelines to help people make decisions.

Lastly, if managers avoid communicating expectations because they don't know what to communicate, then the rest of this chapter should help. But before we move on, one question needs to be answered: When managers avoid setting expectations, where and from whom do employees get them? They get them from many different sources.

The most influential source of employee expectations is the behavior of other employees, including managers. From observing behaviors people make the assumption that if it is permissible for one person then it must be permissible for everyone. When people develop their own set of expectations based on observed behavior, they will often reinforce the expectations which satisfy their needs and not necessarily those in the best interest of the organization. That is human nature.

Employees can also develop their expectations from previous managers. This can be good or bad, depending on the previous manager's ability to set expectations that meet organizational needs.

People also bring into the workplace their cultural background, work history and personal beliefs. These factors also influence expectations.

If managers do not set clear expectations, people will develop their own set of assumptions. In Bob's example, he may believe he did everything in his power to meet expectations that he assumed were correct. If his manager did not clarify and obtain agreement to the expectations beforehand, Bob won't feel responsible, nor will he hold himself accountable.

Two Types of Expectations

In the corporate world, expectations fall into two categories: standards and goals. Standards are general expectations of conduct that help businesses to function in an efficient manner. Examples of standards include work hours, drug and alcohol policy and vacation policy. Goals stretch the organization to move into the future. Standards are processed-focused. Goals are future-focused.

In a results-driven culture, goals receive more emphasis than standards. But goals without standards become de-motivating. When managers neglect the process of identifying and coming to agreement on standards, they overlook the first step in facilitating the learning process.

As previously stated, standards can be perceived as rules and regulations or boundaries. The more a manager sees his or her job as controlling behavior, the more likely he or she is to dictate or avoid setting standards. Often this type of manager will try to extrinsically motivate people to change unproductive behavior through goal setting.

Standards

The first responsibility a manager has to his or her people is to communicate and agree upon clear standards. Standards are general expectations of conduct that help to facilitate business processes and decisions. Standards establish boundaries within which employees can make decisions. Standards address day-to-day activities and how people conduct themselves.

Unlike goals, employees are not rewarded for meeting standards. If the standards are agreed upon, realistic and measurable, then people are held accountable to them. Without clear standards it is impossible and unfair to hold people accountable.

A manager helps create an environment for learning by coming to agreement on a code of conduct with his or her employees. Managers will have the most success holding people accountable to standards that are realistic, measurable and agreed upon.

Expectations need to be realistic if people are going to buy into them. People will not hold themselves accountable nor feel responsible for unrealistic expectations. If management defines expectations that are unrealistic, management will be responsible for holding people accountable. If employees do not buy into expectations, management will be forced to use an autocratic behaviorist approach to keep employees "in line."

Another characteristic of effective expectations is measurability. Expectations that can be readily observed and measured make sense to employees and help build a foundation for learning. An ambiguous standard can de-motivate employees, especially if the manager is responsible for defining what behavior falls within the standard.

For example, let's say a standard exists for all employees to have a good attitude. If the manager is the judge of what is or isn't considered a good attitude, then employees will feel that they have little control over what behaviors fall within the desired standard. This can de-motivate. A better standard might be for people to leave their personal problems out of business discussions.

Agreement on standards is the key difference between autocratic behaviorism and facilitative leadership. Managers who believe they are "in charge" will most often define and communicate standards to their people. Excluding people from control over rules they are expected to live by will affect the amount of responsibility they take for them. By forcing standards on people, managers get compliance but rarely commitment.

Standards can be broken down into formal and informal. Formal standards are rules to ensure a safe, effective company environment while informal standards are the tools managers can use to facilitate the learning process.

Formal Standards

Formal standards are defined either by the company or by government regulations and apply to the entire organization. An example of a formal company standard may be standardized work hours. A formal government standard is the OSHA requirement to wear hard hats in construction sites. Formal standards establish a safe and effective corporate environment within which all employees must operate.

Formal standards are usually codified and printed in a company handbook. It is the company's responsibility and the individual manager's to ensure that all employees are aware of these standards.

Managers can communicate formal standards as rules and regulations or as boundaries identified by the company and government to facilitate processes and protect people. While managers have little direct control over formal standards, they can control how they are communicated.

Informal Standards

Informal standards are the boundaries an individual manager and his or her employees have identified as necessary to accomplish day-to-day tasks. They are within the manager's span of control. Informal standards are best defined and agreed to collaboratively by the people who are expected to live by them. Informal standards help build an environment that reflects the department's business and personal values. Examples include guidelines for holding meetings, how conflicts are resolved and general communication ground rules.

While job descriptions are individual standards and define <u>what</u> is expected of employees, informal standards define <u>how</u> employees are expected to fulfill their responsibilities in the context of working with others.

It is a manager's responsibility to ensure that all of his or her employees understand and agree to these standards. Managers ultimately have the authority to define and implement standards, but in order to encourage people to make their own decisions it is critical that managers get their people to help define and agree to standards.

An autocratic behaviorist manager will dictate standards he or she feels are important without getting input from the people who are expected to live by them. A facilitative leader lets his or her group define the most important areas in which standards facilitate work processes. Then he or she allows the people affected by the standard work out the guidelines to improve these processes.

In order to collaboratively define standards it is critical to know the difference between rules and boundaries.

Rules Vs. Boundaries

Most managers see standards as hard and fast rules which they are supposed to enforce. Facilitative leaders see them as boundaries to guide decision making. The purpose of rules is to control. The purpose of boundaries is to guide.

Rules are normally set in the context of what isn't allowed without any indication of what is allowed. They have a tendency to limit the amount of judgment a person has to use to evaluate compliance to the rule. Rules limit the choice to either compliance or non-compliance.

Boundaries allow judgment and choice by the person expected to live within them. Broad boundaries give people a wider range of choices and therefore people will have to exercise more judgment. Narrow boundaries provide less choice and judgment.

Formal standards are more likely to be set as hard and fast rules because the consequences of violating them can have an severe impact on others. A strict Drug and Alcohol policy is an example of a formal standard in the form of a rule. The consequences of an employee showing up to work under the influence of drugs or alcohol and then operating heavy machinery can be severe. Some rules are necessary to ensure that a business functions properly.

But too many unnecessary rules can interfere with a manager's ability to be effective. Using effective boundaries instead of rules in certain situations may save a manager time and help employees learn. Informal standards are the best tools managers have to help people become better at making decisions.

We can use a parenting analogy to illustrate how a standard can be used in a way to help people learn. Parents who see their primary responsibility as ensuring that their children obey may define a rule like, "No bike riding in the street." This only tells the child what he or she cannot do. Using this rule when the child rides into the street, the parent will hold the child accountable by taking away his or her bike riding privileges. This is seen by the child as punishment.

Parents who see their primary responsibility as helping children learn will define boundaries like, "You may ride your bike in the driveway until you can ride without falling down. Then you can ride in the street." The child will then practice learning how to ride before approaching the parent to ride in the street. Which approach will the child be more motivated to follow?

In the first example, the parent will spend time monitoring whether or not the child is in the street. In the second, the parent will spend time tracking the child's learning process.

A comparison can be drawn between the parent and the manager. Telling employees what they can and cannot do affects their motivation. When they have boundaries within which they can make decisions, they may be more likely to motivate themselves.

Below are examples of how an informal standard can be defined as a rule or a boundary:

Rule:

"All meetings will start on time regardless of the excuse."

Boundary:

> *"Meetings will start at the published time regardless of whether all attendees are present. Anyone showing up late will be responsible for coming up to speed without interfering with the meeting's progress."*

This gives people the choice to show up late, understanding that choice has added responsibilities.

Rule:

> *"Yelling at or threatening another employee is inexcusable."*

Boundary:

> *"People are expected to try to resolve issues they have with their co-workers before escalating the issue to their manager. The process of resolving issues must be done with respect for each other. If conflict becomes difficult to manage the issue can be brought to a manager's attention. Employees are expected to use their best judgment."*

By stating this standard in the form of a boundary, a manager provides the employee more

control and discourages unnecessary escalation
of trivial issues.

Rule:

> *"E-mail is to be used for necessary
> communication only."*

Boundary:

> *"The E-mail system may not be used to
> communicate missed deadlines, critical
> customer issues, tardiness excuses or
> anything that has a critical response
> time attached to it. Use your best judg-
> ment."*

This better defines what is and isn't "necessary
communication" but leaves room for employees to make their own decisions.

Rule:

> *"Employees must meet deadlines."*

Boundary:

> *"If an employee determines he or she
> cannot meet a deadline, this must be
> communicated to the involved parties
> including managers as soon as the bar-
> rier to meeting the deadline is encoun-
> tered. Use your best judgment."*

Once again the employee has some control over the process.

Standards defined and communicated as boundaries give people some control over their lives. This makes the standard more effective in the end. People who feel they have some control over their environment are more likely to motivate themselves.

Effectiveness of Standards

The most critical element that impacts a standard's effectiveness is the manager's commitment to live within it. Whether managers like it or not, they become authority figures to the people they manage. With this increased authority goes the increased responsibility to set an example by living within the same boundaries as their people. Managers who violate a standard but continue to hold others accountable to that same standard are not being fair. This point must be taken into account when determining whether a standard is realistic. Managers who believe standards only apply to their people and not to themselves lose respect from employees. With the loss of respect goes a corresponding loss of influence of both the manager and the standard.

Arbitrary application of a standard also impacts its effectiveness. Managers who apply a standard when it is convenient or apply it selectively when they want to change a specific person's behavior impact the standard's effec-

tiveness. They also impact their ability to manage. Evenhanded application of standards to
both employees and managers greatly increases
their effectiveness. Equitable application of
standards strengthens accountability to them.

Setting and getting people to buy into expectations without controlling is more art than sci-
ence. Employees are more likely to buy into an
expectation if they believe it facilitates employee and company success and they have
some control over the process of setting expectations.

Managers who control often avoid setting clear
expectations or dictate the standards they think
are important. A facilitative leader communi-
cates and gets agreement upon realistic, measurable standards that are important to help the
employee and company move forward. Managers who see themselves as superior to their
employees will define informal standards as
rules and regulations. Managers who see that
their role is to help people become better decision makers will collaboratively set expectations as boundaries within which everyone is
expected to operate.

Bob is violating a formal standard when he shows up late to work. He is violating an informal standard when he doesn't return voice mail messages or gives incomplete information if the standard has been communicated and agreed upon. The first step in turning Bob's performance around is to make sure he understands and buys into the formal and informal standards. A manager using an autocratic approach might simply tell Bob he must do things by the book, "or else."

Standards Vs. Goals

Formal standards are the foundation laid by the organization to facilitate processes and protect people. Informal standards overlay formal standards and create an environment within which people can feel safe to make decisions. Without this foundation, goals can be de-motivating. Without a safe base camp it becomes difficult for people to push themselves to greater heights.

Managers who are good at goal setting but poor at clarifying standards often end up with employees who are reticent to accept challenging goals. When an employee has a difficult time determining whether he or she is doing a good job on a day-to-day basis, it is natural to be reticent to accept the increased responsibility of goals. Managers who are good at goal setting will often try to resolve a non-performance issue by setting a goal for the employee to improve. This type of manager might try to "motivate" Bob to improve his punctuality by setting a goal for him to go one month without being late. Bob will accurately perceive this as an attempt to control.

Managers who have set a good foundation of standards have also set the stage for good goals.

Goals

Goals stretch employees and are aligned with some company or departmental objective. A standard sets the boundaries within which goals are achieved. A goal is future-based; a standard is process-based. A goal is concerned with where the person, company or department is going. A standard is concerned with how to get there.

The best goals have the same characteristics as standards; they are agreed upon, realistic, and measurable. But goals have one additional characteristic: a beginning and an end. They are future-focused.

The problem Bob had with his goal of introducing two new products to the market was caused by unclear standards, not poor goals. Good goals always have standards attached to them. Bob's excuse for missing the product introduction because he didn't get the information on time from market research could have been prevented by setting a standard. The standard might be that employees must notify management in advance if they encounter a barrier to achieving a goal. Standards help clarify the process of reaching goals and help employees manage their own progress towards achieving goals.

Below are some examples of good goals that may be ineffective without standards:

Good goal:

"Improve average response time to customer inquiries from 8 hours to 6 hours by year-end." (Rational and may be realistic, but realize that implementation of this goal without a quality standard may result in quicker but poorer quality responses.)

Good goal:

"Implement plan to hold weekly meetings with Marketing department by end of first quarter." (Sounds good, but once again a quality standard will prevent weekly meetings that are unnecessary.)

It becomes obvious that a manager who is good at goal setting can still encounter problems when people achieve the goal but miss the point.

Expectations and Facilitative Leadership

Expectations can be broken down into three areas: formal and informal standards, and goals. Each is a block in the process of building an environment in which people learn to self-manage. Without formal standards, informal standards become irrelevant. Without formal and informal standards, goals become de-motivating.

When employees have a strong foundation of standards and well-written goals, they often motivate themselves. Facilitative leaders set guidelines which allow people to manage themselves. They get themselves out of the way and help people do their work. They facilitate employee motivation.

A manager's job is to help define the boundaries within which employees can achieve goals and grow. Failing to do so results in lost time due to corrective action or re-clarification of standards.

The problem Bob has may be the result of unclear expectations. It is his manager's responsibility to clarify and get agreement before trying to hold him accountable.

Autocratic Behaviorism	**Facilitative Leadership**
· Emphasis on goals	· Emphasis on standards
· Sets standards as rules	· Sets standards as boundaries
· Uses goals to motivate	· Builds foundation for motivation
· Dictates standards & goals	· Seeks consensus on expectations

Feedback

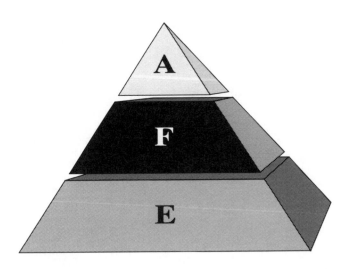

Chapter 3:

Feedback

*Does Bob know he is or is not
meeting expectations?*

In the initial meeting, Bob and his manager
clarified and agreed to expectations. The
next step in helping Bob solve his performance problem is to provide him regular, frequent feedback on his progress. When asked
how he received feedback from his previous
manager, Bob said he received input mostly
when he screwed up. His manager would point
out what he was doing wrong and tell Bob how
to fix the problem. He called it "constructive
criticism."

Sometimes his manager would get frustrated
and complain that Bob wasn't motivated. Bob
insisted he was motivated but had his own way
of doing things. Occasionally, when Bob did a
good job his manager would stop by his office

and tell him to "keep up the good work." Bob appreciated this input but suspected his manager was looking for reasons to compliment him.

The notes in Bob's personnel file indicated that Bob was unmotivated and unresponsive to either praise or criticism. To correct the situation, Bob was given a goal to attend two seminars: one to improve interpersonal skills and one to improve time management. It was also documented that Bob and his manager had formal meetings to motivate him to correct the negative behaviors.

Bob's overall opinion was that the main purpose of his manager's feedback was to get him to fall in line. He complained that his manager spent more time correcting him after the mistake than trying to help him understand how to prevent it.

Bob and his manager were frustrated because the feedback used in their interactions was primarily results-based: praise for a job well done and criticism for one done poorly. Both praise and criticism are forms of results-based feedback.

The alternative to relying solely on praise and criticism is to use encouragement. Encouragement is process-based feedback. Managers who attempt to control behavior use praise and criticism to get people to do what they want them to do. Praise and criticism are other parts of an extrinsic motivation system based upon reward and punishment. Encouragement helps people learn how to manage their own behavior. Using encouragement in place of praise or criticism facilitates the process of learning to make better decisions.

Praise and Criticism as Feedback

Feedback in the form of praise or criticism is another attempt to control behavior through a system of rewards and punishments. Praise is a reward for good performance while criticism is punishment for poor performance. A reward and punishment system is inherently control-based because the recipient of the feedback must be praised or criticized _by_ someone. In business, a manager makes an evaluation of a behavior and provides the employee with feedback. The evaluation is done extrinsically or outside of the employee, and he or she is the recipient of the praise or criticism. This type of feedback is "done" to the employee.

Because this type of feedback is "done" by a manager to an employee, it makes that manager responsible for the behavior and the manager has to "manage" it. It produces compliance, but rarely commitment. Praise and criticism are attempts to motivate through external evaluation and social control. They reinforce the employees' belief that success is dependent upon their manager's evaluation, not their own.

In a management environment that depends mostly on praise and criticism, employees usually perform well as long as their manager keeps up the praise. They often become de-motivated in the process of receiving criticism. These approaches build management-dependent behavior.

Managers who rely on praise and criticism may believe they are managing the progress of the individual, when in fact they are trying to manage results. This type of feedback is easy to do because managers need only pay attention to the end result, not the process. Therefore it takes less time and energy. What managers eventually get from using this type of feedback are employees that are dependent on their manager to determine their success. Using praise and criticism manages dependency into people. Once again, this is reinforced by the "just do it" management culture.

Encouragement

Managers who want to facilitate learning use encouragement to help people manage their own behavior. They realize employees are fallible and focus on the process of improvement, not accomplishment. When managers encourage, they concentrate on the process and progress towards the end result. Managers facilitate achievement by identifying the end goal and managing the progress towards the result. Encouragement is part of a process-based management approach.

Encouragement is a tool to help people manage their own progress. It helps managers to separate the individual from the act. Managers who use this type of feedback see employees as works-in-progress and respect the individual as having inherent self-worth independent of his or her behaviors. Encouragement focuses on people's improvement and their assets and strengths. Praise focuses on past performance and criticism on blame.

The word encouragement comes from the Latin root "coure" meaning heart. The act of using encouragement is meant to help people have the heart or "courage" to make decisions for themselves; to self-manage.

Managers who rely solely on praise and criticism usually see their people as sets of isolated behaviors engaged in achieving results for the manager or company. Good managers see their people as works-in-progress struggling to get better all the time. It is the manager's responsibility to help with this struggle.

Another reason managers get frustrated with employees who are not performing is because managers are usually measured by achievement and end results. This short-term focus promotes linear thinking and the tendency to try to manage and celebrate <u>only</u> results.

To the individual, incremental improvement is more motivating than some externally defined end result. Encouragement recognizes this fact and helps people learn to see the incremental improvements and corrections for themselves. It helps people manage their own progress through self-evaluation. Managers who rely solely on praise and criticism are not managing; they are trying to control.

Discouragement?

Is discouragement the opposite of encouragement? Actually, while encouragement is an active process, discouragement can be the passive result of the process of encouragement. By encouraging certain positive behaviors a person discourages negative ones.

The difference might best be understood by determining the intended purpose of the feedback. If a person wants to reinforce a certain productive behavior, he or she will encourage that behavior. If a person wants to correct a negative behavior, he or she does so by encouraging the desired alternative positive behavior.

People who try to discourage behavior may be using the term to take the edge off of "constructive criticism."

Praise and Criticism vs. Encouragement

Bob's previous manager used primarily the praise/criticism approach to try and motivate Bob. Words like "Great job" and "Keep up the good work" are praise-words. They occur after the fact and refer to past behavior. They are specific only to the desired result. Managers who pay primary attention to the bottom line are usually good at praise and criticism.

Praise to an employee who is not feeling good about his or her performance can further de-motivate. Employees who perceive their manager as authoritarian will see this type of feedback as a thinly veiled attempt to control. Employees often interpret this feedback as a put-down, and identify toeing the line as "giving in" to the manager.

Criticism is an attempt to control by enforcing obedience to rules. Words like "You did it again" or "You should have done it this way" are criticism. Most managers avoid giving criticism until it is too late; they are then perceived as trying to get people to "fall in line."

Encouragement shows employees that managers have respect and confidence in their ability to manage their own behavior. It recognizes effort and incremental improvement. Encouragement takes into account a person's imperfection and struggle to improve. Encouragement is not dependent on achieving an end result, only on effort. It can be applied in process.

Encouragement focuses on behavior and avoids value judgments. The process of using encouragement is participatory and requires managers pay attention and realize that the more they try to control, the more they might negatively impact a person's motivation.

Encouragement can be broken down into two different sets of steps depending on the manager's objectives in the encouragement process. There are two slightly different approaches: one to reinforce positive behavior and another to correct negative behavior.

Encouragement to Reinforce Positive Behavior

The process of encouraging to reinforce positive behavior can be broken down into three steps:

Choose:

Before you sit down with an employee, choose the specific behavior you want to reinforce and limit your feedback to that specific behavior. Also decide what you are going to say and how you are going to say it. As an example, let's say you recently sat through a presentation by one of your employees who did an excellent job of presenting an organized outline that was easy to follow. You will want to prepare to encourage the behavior of providing the outline.

Set Tone:

Because most people naturally become defensive when their manager approaches, it is important to set the tone of the interaction before encouraging. Using the example above, a manager might set the tone by stating, *"I thought the presentation went well."* People will be more open to encouragement when a positive tone is set.

Spike:

To increase the retention of the positive behavior, a manager must spike the delivery by specifically pointing out the positive behavior <u>and</u> the impact on productivity. Instead of saying *"You did a good job of providing an outline,"* a manager could spike the statement by saying, *"I saw you do a particularly good job of organizing and presenting an ordered outline. I think this helped people follow you better and increased the effectiveness of your presentation."* This second statement is more specific and shows the manager is paying attention to process and the results.

A manager may want to end this encouragement with a question such as "What do you think?" It is critical not to let the employee turn the interaction into a discussion about what he or she could do to improve. Mixing the positive message with needs for improvement will lessen the impact of the encouragement.

Encouragement to Correct Negative Behavior

The process for encouraging to correct negative behavior starts off faster, but more time is required at the back end with the addition of a problem-solving step.

Choose:

Using the same presentation example, let's say a manager had previously clarified the expectation that all presentations must start with an overview of the purpose and agenda for the benefit of the attendees. This manager just finished sitting in on an employee's presentation in which no agenda and purpose were covered. Prior to setting the tone, the manager must choose whether to reinforce something the employee did well or correct the negative behavior. Once the manager has decided to correct the negative behavior, he or she must choose how to set the tone, spike and problem solve. The preparation step when correcting negative behavior is more critical than when encouraging positive behavior.

Set Tone:

Most people want bad news quickly without beating around the bush. This manager might start out by saying *"Something concerned me about the presentation."* This helps prepare the employee for the next point.

Spike:

At this point the manager must be firm and matter-of-fact. The specific behavior <u>and</u> it's impact must be delivered with as little personal judgment as possible. *"The presentation started out without a purpose and agenda. This limited the presentation's effectiveness."*

Problem Solve:

At this point the manager should avoid all excuses. If the expectation was realistic, measurable and agreed upon then the manager can validate without accepting. For example, if the employee says he or she was too busy, the manager might reply, *"I know we are all very busy, but we all agreed to starting our presentations this way."* Then proceed to a problem solving step by saying, *"How can you prevent this from happening in future presentations?"*

It is imperative that the manager is careful to keep himself or herself out of the equation. Instead of saying, "I don't like the presentation starting that way," the manager must default to the standard by saying, *"The expectation we agreed upon was…"* The more collaboratively a manager sets standards, the easier it is to keep himself or herself out of the way.

Below are additional examples of autocratic feedback and encouragement using Bob's performance challenges:

Situation:

> Bob completes a lengthy report within a specific time frame and meets all standards.

Praise:

> *"Great job, Bob. Keep up the good work."*

Encouragement to reinforce positive behavior:

> *" Thanks for getting the report done on time, Bob. That really helps our organization look good to other departments."*

Situation:

> Bob doesn't get the job in on time but meets the standards.

Praise/Criticism:

> *"Hey, Bob, nice job on the report. Next time make sure you get it to me on time."*

Encouragement to correct negative behavior:

"You made a lot of progress in the quality of your reports. We can get even better leverage from other departments if we get them in on time. How can I help you do that?"

Encouragement Principles

There are principles that, when applied to the process of encouragement, make the message more effective.

Focus on one behavior:

Managers have a tendency to try and give as much feedback as possible when they have the attention of the employee. This can overwhelm the employee. A manager will be most effective by concentrating on one behavior at a time.

Separate positive from negative:

Realize that mixing negative and positive feedback invalidates the positive and lessens the impact of the negative. If a manager's intention is to correct negative behavior, he or she can include some positives after the problem solving step, but spike the main message of the behavior to correct. If a manager wants to reinforce positive behavior, including any negative behavior will wipe out the desired reinforcement of the positive.

Involve the employee:

Whenever possible, encouragement should be a process that involves the person being encouraged. One effective way is to start with a question like *"I thought the presentation went well. How do you think it went?"* A manager who starts with a question must be sure to spike the behavior.

Initially, a change in a manager's form of feedback from praise and criticism to encouragement will be perceived with suspicion by employees. The only way to relieve this uneasiness is consistent use of an encouragement approach.

When Can a Manager Use Praise or Criticism?

There are situations where praise/criticism feedback is appropriate. Praise can be a genuine expression of accomplishment and gratitude. Criticism can be a sincere attempt to provide information to help turn a person around.

Praise is best used to recognize significant progress or to celebrate large successes. Criticism is best used to address chronic slippage and indifferent behavior. The effective use of praise or criticism is based upon the underlying motivations of the manager and employee. If the manager's motivation is to control no matter how praise or criticism is delivered, the employee will feel controlled. If the employee is motivated by a need to "please" the manager then she or he might become dependent on praise and use it in a subtle way to try and control the manager.

Feedback and Facilitative Leadership

Feedback can be delivered in two ways. Praise and criticism have a place, but are seen by employees as attempts to control. Encouragement focuses on the process of meeting expectations and achieving goals. Employees see an encouragement approach as one of collaboration and mutual respect.

Facilitative leaders recognize and encourage progress and improvement. They don't see people as sets of behaviors. Rather they see them as works-in-progress. A manager who focuses exclusively on the end result is not managing. A hallmark of an autocratic behaviorist approach is an over reliance on praise and criticism to manage behavior. Employees see this as controlling and demanding obedience.

As long as managers see that their primary job is to hold people accountable for reaching objectives, they will see people either as achieving or not achieving. The facilitative leader's job is to help people become more responsible. He or she does so through building trust and confidence by helping employees see the incremental improvements in their abilities. Managers that neglect to give frequent feedback or rely solely on giving praise and criticism are not managing.

In order to use encouragement properly, managers must pay attention to people's behaviors and progress as well as the bottom line. Using this approach helps managers to build their employees' confidence. The goal of a manager is to develop employees' self-management skills, and to help people become responsible decision makers.

Managers owe and are owed frequent feedback. Those who rely on praise and criticism are not managing people; they are trying to manage results. It is unfair when managers withhold feedback but expect good performance.

Bob's second problem stems from his manager's attempt to "motivate" him to achieve results. A facilitative leader will work with Bob in an attempt to build his confidence.

Praise/Criticism	**Encouragement**
· Done <u>to</u> employees	· Done <u>with</u> employees
· Past/present focus	· Present/future focus
· Recognizes achievement	· Recognizes progress
· Focuses on results	· Focuses on process
· Builds management-dependent behavior	· Helps people self-manage

Accountability

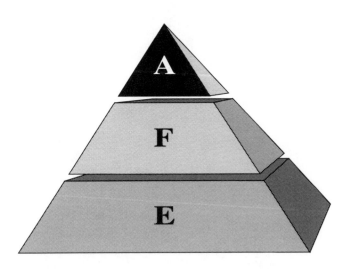

Chapter 4:

Accountability

Has Bob experienced the conse-
quences of his behavior?

Now that Bob is clear on what is expected and has received feedback from
you, what do you do if he continues to
fall back into his old patterns of non-performance? His previous manager avoided dealing
with Bob's problems until they impacted other
employees' performance and could not be
avoided. When forced to confront Bob, his
previous manager threatened disciplinary action or shifted Bob's responsibilities so he
would have less impact on others. When Bob
did respond well and perform, he received
praise and was sometimes rewarded with a
little time off.

Bob consistently showed up late for meetings.
In an attempt to correct this behavior, his man-

ager reminded Bob every time he was late. After many attempts Bob was reprimanded. His manager complained how frustrating it was that Bob knew what was expected but continued his poor behavior.

The next time Bob showed up at a meeting on time, his manager made a point of reinforcing this behavior by thanking him. Bob responded well for a short while but after time slipped back into his old behavior of showing up late. It seemed as though his manager's attempts to hold him accountable had little long-term effect on Bob's behavior. Bob eventually did whatever he wanted, came to expect a reward for performing and became apathetic when faced with punishment. In despair his manager documented the behavior in Bob's personnel file. Finally, Bob's manager avoided dealing with the problem by transferring him to another department; yours.

Bob's previous manager was frustrated mainly because Bob did not respond to attempts to hold him accountable through reward and punishment. Rewards and punishments are tools used by managers to control. This approach works in a system when the person in power is assumed to have the right answer; it de-motivates when people have choices.

Rewards and punishments are seen by employees as attempts to make them conform to the rules. Their reaction is often resistance or grudging compliance. Rarely is it motivation.

Accountability Vs. Reward and Punishment

Using a system of rewards and punishments does not necessarily make people more accountable; it can make them less. Rewards and punishments are one way for managers to hold their people accountable. An alternative is to help people hold themselves accountable.

Managers that use reward and punishment systems mistakenly assume that by holding people accountable they can make them more responsible. No person can make another more responsible. Managers often try to give responsibility to people who don't want to take responsibility. People can be given responsibility without taking responsibility.

Let's define some terms. Responsibility is the degree to which a person or group is accountable for the consequences of their decisions. People can be held accountable, they can hold themselves accountable or both. Taking responsibility is an internal decision people make to hold themselves accountable for the consequences of their actions. Before people will take responsibility, they must have confidence in their ability to take a good course of action.

The logical connection managers make is that they can make people more responsible by holding them more accountable. That is control. People take responsibility when they choose to hold themselves accountable. That is self-management.

A person chooses to become more responsible by accepting the accountability. The degree to which a person holds himself or herself accountable defines the degree to which they feel responsible. Facilitative leaders create opportunities for people to accept responsibility.

How does a manager facilitate accountability? People will accept accountability and take responsibility if they have some control over and confidence in the choices they make. When people have no input into what they will be held responsible for, they naturally avoid being held accountable. When they have some control and are confident in their ability to make good decisions, they will accept responsibility. They then choose to hold themselves accountable and self-manage. People become more responsible as they begin to hold themselves accountable for the consequences of their decisions.

Holding people accountable builds management-dependent behavior because the locus of control is outside the individual. For example, a parent who tries to control will put a glass of juice in front of a child and tell him or her, "Don't spill it." When the child spills the juice the parent will yell at the child and tell him or her, "If you do that again I'm going to send you to bed without dinner." This is an example of using reward and punishment as a means to hold the child accountable. The child quickly learns to depend on the parent to determine what is a good choice and what is a bad choice. The behaviors become parent-dependent. The focus of control is outside of or extrinsic to the child. The child doesn't learn to hold himself or herself accountable.

On the other hand, another parent might clarify the expectation by telling the child that if the juice is spilt then he or she will have to clean it up and refill the glass. When the child spills the juice, he or she experiences the direct consequences of the actions. The child makes the decision based upon the consequences of the behavior, not the consequences delivered by the parent. The child will learn to monitor and manage his or her own behavior. The parent who is holding his or her child "accountable" spends more time "parenting" or controlling short-term behavior.

Managers who use reward and punishment as consequences, like parents who try to control, actually inhibit the ability of an employee to take responsibility. By trying to get an employee to make better decisions a manager makes him or her dependent on the manager to define what is or is not a good decision.

Good managers facilitate the opportunities for employees to experience the direct consequences of their decisions. They facilitate opportunities to learn.

The three tools facilitative leaders have to help people become more responsible are feedback, strategic non-intervention and choice of consequences. The underlying groundwork that supports these tools is clear expectations. These tools, along with clear expectations, help employees to move along the responsibility continuum.

The Responsibility Continuum

Many managers make quick judgments that their people are either responsible or irresponsible. This is another effect of our "just do it" culture. The facilitative leader sees people as works-in-progress along the Responsibility Continuum.

Less Responsible	More Responsible
Given responsibility	Take responsibility
Make poor decisions	Make good decisions
Held accountable	Hold themselves accountable
Management-dependent behavior	Self-management
Narrow boundaries	Broader boundaries

The goal of a facilitative leader is to help a person move from less responsible to more responsible; to help employees hold themselves accountable. When a person is in the process of developing a sense of responsibility, it is necessary for a manager to define narrower boundaries for making choices in order to ensure business progress. People who are more responsible can make more choices because they and their managers have more faith in their ability to make good decisions. A person who is further along on the Responsibility Continuum can have broader boundaries within which he or she can make decisions.

As stated before, the three tools a manager has to move a person along this continuum are feedback, strategic non-intervention and choice of consequences.

Feedback

Feedback in the form of encouragement helps people move along the Responsibility Continuum. Praise and criticism focus on achievement and non-achievement after the fact. Encouragement focuses on progress and future improvement. By design encouragement helps people become more confident in their ability to make choices and take responsibility.

The purpose of encouragement is to build courage. When managers use encouragement they are automatically helping people to make better choices. A manager using praise and criticism may be preventing people from learning how to make their own decisions.

Strategic Non-Intervention

Another tool managers have for facilitating learning is the concept of strategic non-intervention. Strategic non-intervention is defined as letting people experience the direct consequences of their decisions, good or bad. People learn best when they experience direct consequences. When a person touches a hot stove he or she experiences the burning sensation and makes the decision never to do that again. Strategic non-intervention lets people experience the direct consequences of their choices.

But strategic non-intervention is just that: strategic. Returning to the analogy of a parent trying to teach a child to ride a bike, the parent may let the child practice in a school yard but not in the street. This is a strategic decision based on the possible consequences. Once the child learns to ride safely in the school yard, then he or she can move to the street.

In order to ensure that the opportunity to learn occurs in a manner which is in the best interest of the employee and the company, the facilitative leader has to evaluate three different strategic criteria before using strategic non-intervention.

The criteria which a manager must use to determine whether to let employees experience the direct consequences of their decisions are:

Ability:

> *What are the chances of the employee making a poor decision?*

> It is the manager's responsibility to match tasks with ability. If the employee has little experience with the task, strategic non-intervention may be inappropriate in this situation.

Impact on Employee:

> *If the employee makes a poor decision, will the direct consequences of that decision inhibit his or her willingness to make future decisions?*

> It is the manager's responsibility to

evaluate the impact on the employee. A manager must evaluate whether the consequences of making a poor decision will negatively impact the willingness of the employee to make future decisions.

Impact on Productivity:

If the employee makes a poor decision, will the learning that occurs from that decision outweigh the short-term loss in productivity?

It is the manager's responsibility to weigh the organizational impact of a poor decision against the learning that might occur for the employee. If the employee learns a valuable lesson but the department misses a crucial deadline then the learning point might be lost.

Let's use a simple example of Bob's tardiness at meetings. In this situation his previous manager got frustrated with him and threatened punishment.

Evaluating these three criteria to determine

whether it is a good idea for Bob to experience the direct consequences of his behavior might go like this:

Ability:

Since Bob has consistently been late to meetings odds are he will repeat the behavior.

Impact on Employee:

The impact on Bob will probably not severely curtail Bob's willingness to make future decisions. Because this is a minor offense the up-side will have more effect than the down-side.

Impact on Productivity:

This is the most critical point. A manager has to be aware of the impact of Bob missing vital information and weigh it against the productivity lost by starting meetings late.

A manager using strategic non-intervention would clarify and get agreement on the expectation that all meetings are to start on time and anyone who is late will have to catch up. The manager would ensure that the meeting started on-time by closing the door to the meeting room and beginning. When Bob shows up late, no special treatment is provided to bring him up to speed. If Bob asks what is going on he is reminded the meeting must progress so as not to waste other people's time. This is done matter-of-factly and without emotion.

After the meeting when Bob comes to his manager to get caught up, the manager makes no special provisions to help him. The material is provided in the format in which his manager has it. If Bob needs more clarification the manager does so when convenient for the manager, not Bob.

At first this might seem a waste of time and unproductive; it maybe necessary, however. One of the greatest challenges a manager faces is letting an employee struggle with the negative consequences of his or her decisions. Because managers want people to succeed they often try to minimize the direct impact of the consequences to the employee. When they do that it may enable the behavior. This is indirectly harmful to the employee. The psychological definition of enabling is "a harmful form of helping." When managers prevent employees from experiencing the pain or pleasure of the consequences of their choices, they take away an opportunity for their employees to learn.

In this example of strategic non-intervention Bob experiences the direct consequences of his actions. Managers that use punishment but "help" Bob out are actually reinforcing his non-performance and attempting to control him. They also contribute to Bob's non-performance.

Henry Kissinger tells a story about an incident that happened when he was advising President Nixon. Kissinger and Nixon were in the Oval Office discussing Middle East negotiations, but could make no progress because Nixon's dog was chewing and barking at the rug. In frustration, Nixon reached into his desk and threw a bone to the dog. Upon seeing this Kissinger said to Mr. Nixon: "Mr. President, you have just taught your dog to chew rugs."

By not letting Bob experience the direct consequences of his tardiness, his manager is teaching him to "chew rugs." Many managers teach their people to "chew rugs" when they don't allow them to experience the direct consequences of their decisions. They are trying to control the amount of discomfort an employee might feel.

Another example of this occurs when managers complain that they cannot get any work done because their people always come into their office to discuss problems. These managers might be reinforcing this behavior by volunteering the answer to the employees' problems.

Managers who control take responsibility for problems that are not theirs and in which employees would actually benefit from making their own judgments. Managers who try to solve personality conflicts between employees are taking responsibility for problems outside of their control. A manager using strategic nonintervention would clarify the expectation that people are to respect each other's right to different opinions but find a way to resolve conflict without violence or yelling. Then the manager would let the employees work it out.

Using the parent analogy, when two kids are fighting and a parent steps in to try and stop the arguing, the children learn to come back to the parent to mediate any disputes. "Johnny said he won't be my friend if I don't do what he wants." A better suggestion is for the parent to say, "If you two want to continue to play together you will have to find a way to get along," and leave it at that. The kids will find a way to get along or suffer the consequences. The parent has clarified the expectation and used strategic non-intervention to let the children decide whether they want to experience the consequences or try to get along on their own.

Because strategic non-intervention is strategic, a manager has to make the critical judgment whether the individual employee is at an appropriate point on the responsibility continuum.

If employees are not ready to hold themselves accountable and are not taking responsibility for their choices, a manager may have to communicate choices that the employee needs to make.

Communicating Choices

When a person continues to under-perform even in the face of clear expectations, good feedback and strategic non-intervention, as a last resort the employee may need to be presented with a choice of consequences. This is a last resort for a facilitative leader because it forces an employee to make a choice. Presenting a choice of consequences without controlling is a challenge.

Many managers avoid confrontation by putting up with chronic behavior or by moving a poorly performing employee to another part of the organization. But if a manager has been responsible to an employee by communicating clear expectations, providing prompt feedback, and allowing the employee to learn <u>and</u> the employee continues to make bad choices, then the employee has chosen to live with the consequences.

The challenge a manager faces is to communicate the choice an employee needs to make from an impersonal, objective point of view.

When it gets to this point in a business relationship, a manager is often frustrated with the employee. In this emotional atmosphere he or she might take a controlling path and threaten punishment. There is a choice, however.

By communicating the logical choice an employee must make, a manager can get out of the way and not control. The employee is ultimately responsible for his or her life and can learn by being given an opportunity to make a choice. There are four steps in communicating a logical choice:

Plan:

It is crucial that the manager identifies what to say and how to say it. Pre-planning helps to relieve some of the stress which naturally goes with this situation. Pre-planning should include self-examination to identify whether the manager has provided expectations and feedback prior to communicating choices.

Set Tone:

Link the expectation and the negative behavior related to the expectation. The language should be firm and terse, and the manager must avoid getting derailed. Using Bob's continued tardiness as an example it might sound like this:

"Bob, everyone is expected to work five days a week from eight to five. You have been late two days in the past month."

Spike:

State the impact the negative behavior is having on the organization's, not the manager's, productivity. The manager can get out of the way by directing the impact away from himself or herself. Continuing with Bob's tardiness example:

"Your tardiness is interfering with the ability of other people to get their work done."

Hand off:

> State the choice the employee must make
> to live within the boundary or live with
> the negative consequences. Using an
> "either, or.." statement provides a clear
> choice. This is not a problem-solving
> step. The manager is handing off the
> choice entirely to the employee.
>
> *"You have a choice. Either you meet the
> punctuality standard or the tardiness will
> be noted in your performance review."*

Being effective when asking an employee to
make a choice of consequences requires self-
control and the ability to separate the person
from the behavior. Guidelines for the effective
communication of choices include being un-
emotional, direct and firm. If a manager has
done a good job of creating an environment in
which this person can succeed but he or she
continues to exhibit the negative behavior, it is
no longer the manager's problem. The intention
of stating the choice of consequences is to
transfer the entire responsibility for making the
choice to the employee. A manager must avoid

being coaxed into problem-solving or listening to excuses. This is not a debate; it is a choice the employee must make.

It quickly becomes obvious that communicating choices is a last resort for managers. Ensuring that clear expectations, feedback and strategic non-intervention precede this step is the key to ensuring that this tactic is fair to the employee. It is critical that choices the employee must make are not related the what the manager wants. It isn't being "done" to the employee by the manager. Rather it is the choice the employee must make to live within the agreed upon expectations of the company.

In this example, Bob's manager is leaving it up to Bob to make the choice. Bob is responsible for the corrective actions. His manager is responsible for ensuring that the negative consequence occurs if Bob chooses to maintain the negative behavior.

Accountability and Facilitative Leadership

Managers who try to make people responsible by holding them accountable fail to realize that this is a disguised attempt to make people conform. People do much better when they choose to take responsibility and hold themselves accountable.

Managers can take two different approaches to holding people accountable. Use of reward and punishment is seen by employees as an attempt to get them to "fall in line." Facilitating the process of taking responsibility allows the manager to get out of the way of an employee's learning. Strategic non-intervention allows the employee to learn by experiencing the direct consequences of his or her own behavior. Choice of consequences teaches by forcing employees to make decisions about their future behavior.

In order for managers to help people accept more responsibility, they need to have a more objective and impersonal perspective of their responsibilities. Managers are not responsible *for* their employees' behavior. They are responsible *to* them by providing expectations, feedback and the opportunities to learn. Managers will have an easier time in the long run if they let their employees work out their own answers to problems.

The facilitative leader realizes people will take responsibility when they feel confident in the choices they make. People gain confidence by having opportunities to make choices and experience the direct consequences. Rewards and punishments are not direct consequences; they are the manager's consequences.

Helping people become responsible is about facilitating the opportunities for people to make choices and learn. It is realizing that people are works-in-progress and that experience is the best teacher. Watching people experience the negative consequences of their choices can be painful. It is pleasant when the consequences are positive. Facilitative leaders detach themselves and find pleasure in the learning that takes place from both types of choices. It can be painful to watch a person learn from bad decisions, but it results in people taking more responsibility for their lives and holding themselves accountable.

A manager's responsibility is to strategically allow people the opportunity to learn. When managers try to make people more responsible through reward and punishment, they are not managing. They are trying to control.

A manager's responsibility is to facilitate learning. There is a fine line between facilitating learning and abdicating responsibility. The difference is attention and involvement. Abdication is passive. Applying the concept of strategic non-intervention, using feedback and choice of consequences is actively managing.

Bob's last problem stems from his manager's attempts to control his behavior through reward and punishment. Bob was deprived of his ability to learn. His manager tried to hold him accountable without allowing him to experience the consequences of his behavior.

Reward & Punishment	Facilitating Responsibility
· Demands compliance	· Presents choices
· Implies moral judgment	· Is objective and impersonal
· Focuses on the past and blame	· Focuses on present and future
· Emphasizes position power	· Emphasizes business standards

Can Facilitative Leadership Work in the American Business Culture?

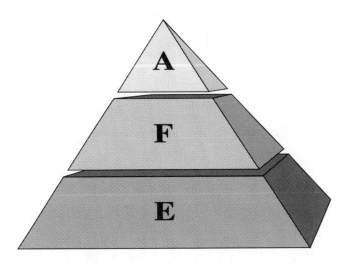

Chapter 5:

Can Facilitative Leadership Work in the American Business Culture?

Another way to pose the question in the title of this chapter is, "Can a process-based management philosophy work in a results-based corporate culture?" The answer to this question can be found by examining a previous attempt to do exactly this.

The "Empowerment" Myth

In the late 80's and early 90's management came to believe that decisions were best made by the people closest to the customer. This was the basis for the "empowerment" movement in corporations in the past decade. Most companies subscribe to this "empowerment" as the best way to service customers.

In response to this belief, managers were encouraged to "empower" their people by giving them more authority to make decisions. Managers became responsible for ensuring that their people took responsibility and made smart decisions. When managers tried to "empower" their people, employees resisted being "empowered." As corporations and managers encountered unexpected difficulties the movement slowed. Corporations, managers and employees became disenchanted with the entire idea.

In frustration, managers frequently sought out consultants, corporate gurus and motivational speakers to help them answer the questions, "How can we get people to make decisions and take responsibility?" and "How can we empower people?" Despite the time and money spent searching for the answers to these questions, it seems that even today the "empowerment" movement is still bogged down.

And the "empowerment" movement will continue to be bogged down until corporations realize that the true answer to the question, "How can we empower people?" is "You can't."

When the "empowerment" philosophy was adopted into our "just do it" corporate culture, the result was a control-based approach to "empowering" people. Managers attempted to do this by giving people more responsibility and holding them accountable for making responsible decisions. The underlying misconception was that managers had the power to make people take responsibility.

As managers tried to give people responsibility they were frustrated because people resisted taking it. They resisted because the methods used to "empower' people were thinly disguised attempts to control and manage results. They were attempts to externally motivate people to hold themselves accountable. In other words, management was trying to extrinsically motivate people to make an intrinsic decision to take responsibility.

True Empowerment

True empowerment occurs when an individual is given <u>and</u> accepts responsibility for a specific task or process by holding <u>himself or herself</u> accountable for the decisions regarding that task or process. Individuals are truly empowered when they make the intrinsic choice to take responsibility for consequences of their decisions.

But management continues to believe that people can be managed into taking responsibility. Management believes people will take responsibility even when they have little control over what is expected from them. When people are not given input into what they are going to be responsible for and held accountable to, why would they take responsibility?

People will take responsibility (or empower themselves) when they have some control over their environment and are confident in their abilities. Managers who attempt to "empower" people by giving them more responsibility and holding them accountable are simply trying to control them. The "empowerment" movement in the American business culture was seen by employees for what it really was: another attempt to manage results and not process.

Managers can help people empower themselves by helping them become responsible decision makers and giving them some control over what is expected from them. Managers can help people take more responsibility by concentrating more on process and less on results.

Which brings us back to this chapter's question, "Can a manager focus on the process of helping people become better decision makers in an environment which reinforces and rewards short-term results?" Put another way, "Can a manager focus on the long-term development of his or her people while still achieving short-term objectives?"

Management Focus Continuum

So far, this book has concerned itself with two
different management approaches. It contrasted
the autocratic behaviorist approach of attempting to achieve results through control to the
facilitative approach of building a solid foundation for people to become better decision
makers. For purposes of illustration, this book
depicted these as two different and separate
management approaches. In fact, most managers play somewhere in between the two. Their
behaviors fall somewhere along the Management Focus Continuum.

MANAGEMENT FOCUS CONTINUUM

Autocratic   **Facilitative**
Behaviorist   **Leader**

|—————————————————————————|

Control short-term   Help people become
behavior   responsible decision
                                             makers

A manager's behavior will fall at different points along this continuum depending on three interdependent factors: the manager's own belief system, corporate pressure and the amount of responsibility an employee is prepared to take.

Manager's Belief System

Managers who believe their job is to control short-term behavior to ensure results will use an autocratic behaviorist approach to manage people. When managers see themselves as being "in charge" of their people, they naturally use autocratic behaviorist approaches. They will use accountability as the main tool to keep people in line.

Managers who believe their job is to help people become better decision makers will use a more facilitative management approach. Their behaviors will be further along the Management Focus Continuum.

The controlling manager is more likely to unilaterally define measurable expectations and hold people accountable. A manager whose focus is facilitating will collaboratively define and get agreement on standards and goals. The latter will set standards as boundaries; the former will set them as hard and fast rules. The autocratic behaviorist approach utilizes results-based feedback in the form of praise and criticism, while the facilitative leader will use process-based encouragement.

A manager's belief system is one of the factors that influences at what point along the Management Focus Continuum their behaviors fall. Another factor is corporate pressure.

Corporate Pressure

In the corporation of the 90's, there is incredible pressure on companies to achieve short-term bottom line results. In the struggle to achieve short-term quarterly profit goals, American corporations have down-sized or "right-sized" to cut costs and increased productivity through technology and better utilization of resources, including human resources.

One of the ways in which companies have increased productivity is through longer work hours and harder work. Workers in the 90's are expected to work longer hours with decreased or at least no relative increase in pay or benefits. Corporations are expecting more and more from employees and offering them less. Many workers believe corporations are expecting too much of them. Management expects people to work more and get less.

This ever-rising demand on employees' time and energy has resulted in unrealistic expectations. People will not hold themselves accountable or take responsibility for unrealistic expectations. They will refuse to be "empowered" in an environment in which they have no say over what and how much is expected of them.

Corporate pressure on managers to get more out of their people forces them to take a short-term controlling approach to get results. The ability of managers to help people become better decision makers runs directly counter to ever-rising demand for more productivity.

Ever-rising expectations can only be satisfied with ever-increasing resources. People's time and energy are limited resources. Management's attempt to "empower" people to take responsibility for unrealistic expectations runs counter to the definition of an "empowered" corporate culture.

This short-term focus drives true empowerment out of the corporation. A manager who wants to succeed in the eyes of the corporation must achieve results. In order to achieve results he or she must get people to perform to unrealistic expectations. When people don't agree to unrealistic expectations the manager is left with the only management tool for this situation: control. In an attempt to manage to the end result, the manager defaults to accountability to get people to fall in line.

The result of this short-term focus is that managers feel they have little choice but to use an autocratic approach to managing. The "just do it" value system unfairly forces managers to adopt a control strategy. The more a company takes a short-term approach to business, the more managers will exhibit autocratic behaviors.

The last factor that influences the approach a manager will take is the employee's ability to take responsibility.

Employee's Ability

The last factor that influences whether a manager's approach is one of control or facilitation is the ability of the employee to handle responsibility. When an employee is new or has a short track history in making decisions, a manager may take a more autocratic approach to decision making. While the approach may be more autocratic, it can still be more guiding than controlling.

The boundaries for a person who is not ready for major responsibilities must be set narrower than a person who is adept at making important decisions. The employee who isn't capable or resists taking responsibility will benefit from more definitive expectations and directive feedback. A more experienced employee can have more say and control over his or her area of responsibility.

These three factors of belief system, corporate pressure and employee ability all influence at what point a manager's behavior will fall along the Management Focus Continuum.

"just do it" just doesn't

At this point it might be easy for a manager to abdicate responsibility for adopting an autocratic behaviorist approach to our results-driven culture. A manager might place the blame for using a controlling management style on the corporate bottom line mentality. While there is ample evidence that corporate culture strongly influences the approach a manager takes, there is an element of personal choice as well.

A manager who makes the choice to begin the transition from an autocratic behaviorist approach to that of a facilitative leader must start by examining his or her belief system. That is the first step for managers in taking responsibility for the part they play in their own management style.

To make the transition from an autocratic behaviorist management approach to that of a facilitative leader, a manager will need to use a combination of results-based and process-based behaviors. Just as employees are making a transition from less responsible to more responsible, managers will need to make the transition from controlling short-term behavior to helping people become better decision makers. For this managers will need time, practice and energy, plus a personal choice to look for longer-term improvement in employee behavior.

A Need for Balance

It is important to point out the critical role corporations play in this process. The drive towards unlimited growth and profits will eventually contribute to a workplace with expectations too high for employees to accept. Making people work in an environment in which they have little choice and ever-rising expectations will result in low employee morale. Morale does impact productivity.

Many workers feel that corporations are out of balance today. From the perspective of the employee, the most important corporate values in the 90's are growth and profits. These values seem to supersede all others. Individual contribution, security, loyalty and employee development become expendable when a company is in danger of missing its quarterly profit goals.

Management has come under increasing criticism for it's inability to "walk its talk." Managers say the most important resource is the human resource, but they continue to put people below the bottom line. Management's behaviors don't support their words. The short-term profit goals always squeeze the long-term development of people. The long-term view is in short supply.

True leaders balance a short- and long-term view of their world. But putting a person at the head of a corporation doesn't make him or her a leader. Being in a position of authority may make a person a leader in his or her own eyes but not in the eyes of their people. The title of leader is earned not in things accomplished but in people developed. The more confidence people feel in themselves, the greater the leader.

This is the paradox: the person who wants to lead will never be a leader. To be a leader, a person must help others lead. To be a leader, a person must be willing to serve others. When a person is helping others to build confidence in themselves, he or she is leading.

Like the orchestra conductor, when a company has low morale, unhappy employees and frustration with management a facilitative leader will look first in the mirror to find solutions to these problems. An autocratic behaviorist will look at the stock price.

ORDER FORM

Qty.	Title	Price	Total
	Facilitative Leadership	$ 14.95 (U.S.)	
		Subtotal	
		Shipping & Handling (add $3.00 for one book, $1.00 for each additional book)	
		Total Enclosed	

Payment Method: Please Check One:

❑ **Cheque** (Payable to Steve Reilly)

❑ **Postal Money Order**

❑ **Credit Card Order:**

    Expiration Date:_____/_____

    ❑ Visa   ❑ Master Card

    Card #:_____ - _____ - _____

    Daytime Phone:_____

    Signature:_____

❑ **FAX orders:**
1-206-784-4529. Fill out
the order blank and fax.

❑ **e mail Orders:**
scg.wolfnet.com

❑ **Internet Orders:**
http://www.wolfenet.com/~scg

Please send to:

Name:_____
Address:_____
City:_____
Providence/State:_____ Postal/Zip Code:_____

STEVE REILLY

7743 - 28th Avenue N.W. • Seattle, WA 98119

Quantity discounts are available.
For more information, call 206-784-4529

Thank you for your order!